Date Due

JUL 0 2 2002		
JUL 0 3 2002		
JUL 0 4 2002		

Mining for Sun

MINING FOR SUN

John Reibetanz

Brick Books

CANADIAN CATALOGUING IN PUBLICATION DATA

Reibetanz, John
  Mining for Sun

Poems.
ISBN 1-894078-07-1

1. Title.

PS8585.E448M56 2000   C811'.54   C99-932968-5
PR9199.3.R44M56 2000

We acknowledge the support of the Canada Council
for the Arts for our publishing programme. The support of
the Ontario Arts Council is also gratefully acknowledged.

The cover image, *Friday Night*, by Robert Kemp, is courtesy
of Barbara Kemp. The author photo is by Timothy Reibetanz.

Typeset in Trump. Stock is acid-free Zephyr Antique laid.
Printed and bound by The Porcupine's Quill Inc.

Brick Books
431 Boler Road, Box 20081
London, Ontario N6K 4G6

brick.books@sympatico.ca

For Julie

CONTENTS

The man led the way through the underground passage into the house, letting the curtain fall in front of the door as he passed, thinking the boy was close behind him. The moment the door flap fell behind the man as he entered, the boy caught up the ball of light and put it in the turned up flap of his fur coat in front; then ... he fled away to the north, running until his feet became tired; then by means of his magic coat he changed into a raven and flew as fast as his wings would carry him. This he continued to do ... until he reached his own village and said, 'Now, you good-for-nothing shamans, you see I have brought back the light.'

– 'Raven Steals the Sun' (Northwest Coast legend)

The real world, the *whole* world, does not consist only of the things *of* which we are conscious; it consists also of the consciousness and subconsciousness that are correlative to them. They are the immaterial component of the world. But today the only immaterial element our mental habit acknowledges is our own little spark of self-consciousness. That is why we feel detached, isolated, cut off not only from the world as it really is, but also from those other little sparks of detached self-consciousness we acknowledge in our fellow human beings.

– Owen Barfield

Baudelaire ... on the very verge of exhaustion and anguish, seems to glimpse a gleam of light and to identify the perishable object, in spite of its profound precariousness, with something precious. This is what he so rightly called the *new sun*.

– Yves Bonnefoy

ONE

An Offering

When a creature dies ... the flesh
and soft parts of the body rot quickly.
All that is left are the bones and teeth.
      (textbook entry on 'fossils')

Sometimes. You, mother,
dying, left what was hard first:
bones weeping into

your veins like flutes, teeth
vanished on some hospital
lunch tray. In your last

mute days you parted
with one more hard thing: the gold
ring I was to save

for my child. As your
hand offered that bright circle
(only seen as a

whole now, when empty)
did your thoughts reach, like mine, for
your first wedding ring?

You took that one off
when I was seven or eight
and sent it spinning

from a car window.
I can still feel the wet blades
of grass slipping through

my fingers, night dew
coming on, you and father
loud in the parked car.

I searched there as if
life spilled from a ring that lay
somewhere out of sight

but within reach, hid
where only the crickets knew.
I took the scraping

of their mating calls
for crying, as if they shared
loss – my childish heart

consoled by a soft
'as if.' The consolation
carries on: their song

(light as air, softer
than voices) plays through my thoughts
about that evening

and fills the lost ring's
hollow with life's most lasting
part, cries for new love.

Kaleidoscope

The world had not yet set:
it shifted and rippled
like wind-dimpled water
or water-curtained wind.

Clothespegged to the wheelframe,
flapping against the spokes,
a playing card became
a motor for a bike.

Toppled over, the tall
rectangular cardboard
box from a just-installed
fridge or washer lumbered

along the ground – our tank
powered by hands and knees
that rode each side's jackknifed
collapse to the pavement.

In stoopball, our batter
was a sandstone step's edge:
rubber balls pitched at it
would bound across the surge

of cars and buses down
four lanes, invisible,
and then – like manna – find
hands cupped for miracles.

I lay in bed one night
and turned over my room
by staring at the white
ceiling until it seemed

a cleared-off, spotless floor;
and as I thought my foot
over the raised doorway,
I saw again the white

chalkline someone had drawn
that afternoon around
my friend, the other John,
who'd curled up on the ground

and looked like sleeping since
a bus caught him before
he'd time to catch my hit.
I wondered how the hard

asphalt had let him pass
through to another world,
where thought's turns rose and rose
like upward waterfalls.

Roseland

We danced the Fragmentation Waltz, my mother
   who'd been dead three years, and me: the hand
that I held first still kept its tremble and the nicotine
   stains at the tips of the first three fingers, and her feet
shuffled fatly across the dark varnished parquet
   of her Manhattan living room in those pink terrycloth
slippers she wore in old age to ease the bunions,

   but without missing a step we glided onto the pier
behind the floating seafood restaurant and I had to wonder
   at how she kept her stiletto heels from getting caught
between the planks, especially since she had to bend
   over slightly to hold me in my sailor suit looking up
at the sweep of her brown hair around the silver earring
   that slipped through into the bay later that night,

but as we spun out the sliding glass doorway onto the garden
   apartment's patio it was harder for me to get a grip
with my right hand around her waist, slightly rubbery
   under the green chiffon blouse that humid evening,
and we followed the music languidly through air thick
   with barbecued spare rib fumes and violins weeping
from speakers mingling and disappearing with the smoke.

From Chedworth Roman Villa, Many Happy Returns

Dear Uncle Chris, welcome back to my mind
    after so many years. Forgive me for
      not thinking you up sooner: the coiled-vine

repeats on these unearthed mosaic floors
    should have been all you needed to slip through
      oblivion, the way a live vine's flowers

escape from undergrowth. Three shades of blue
    spun the same triple braid in small square tiles
      winding over the kitchen table where you

inlaid blue-petalled limestone flowers – a child's
    dream garden, planted with such solid faith
      this child's muscles couldn't move it an inch.

We roamed it after meals. You taught me the braid's
    name among tilesetters, *guilloche*, your tongue
      loving the sounds as it still loved the brandy

that drove Aunt Helen away before I was born,
    and left you thirsting after summer guests
      for your big house by the water at Cold Spring.

* * *

Today, it took the eyes of Spring herself
    in warm brown tile to summon you. She ran
      naked towards me, silk scarf beneath her breasts

floating outstretched before her like a ribbon
    at a race she was about to win, only
      the thin glaze holding her back in Roman Britain.

Her eyes escaped, artlessly breaking free –
    the tiles a 'simple provincial product' too
      big for her head. Their emptiness pulled me

back to the first time I had ever seen you
  without your bottle-glass-thick lenses, put
    away for safety by the nurse. Brown pools

deep enough to drown in – you had tried it,
  giving up quick swigs for the long, unbroken
    indraft of madness – emptied by shock treatments,

every glimmer of recognition gone.
  Your eyes' light would return; your trembling hands
    could never weave those tile ribbons again.

                    * * *

The ribbons only seem to pass under
  each other and come up again: *guilloche*,
    the 'universal repeat,' is not three bands

spiralling in one long embrace. Our wish
  for endlessness spins endless rounds of thread
    from isolated sets of flat square chips.

Our longing eyes soften the tile's knife-edge
  to curve: they warm stone out of torpor, couple
    separateness, and bring life to the dead

mineral, the lost woman, the loved uncle.
  It is our thirst that sets these waters flowing,
    dream-blue and body-warm, undrinkable:

unlike the waters running from the spring
  you showed me once, that gave your town its name.
    We knelt over a gap between stones, filling

empty milk bottles with a leaping gleam.
  Held up, it looked like nothing; but my tongue,
    tasting, met fangs that bit deep, and went numb.

The Cutting Board

for David, coming of age

The hardest skill you learned this year needed
no circuitry – neither the wired kind
of labyrinth connected to a keyboard,
nor mortal coils where words and numbers wind
and burrow through the uplands of the mind.

This was a more straightforward mystery:
primitive lining-up of eye and hand,
object as old and solid as a tree.

Sharp metal taught you, through your fingertips,
respect for distance, deference towards knot
and grain. You learned how hard simplicity

and straightness are to make when all you've got
are grown-up tools, heavy, awkward to wield.

Your skinned hands toughened as they smoothed the wood.

First Frost

Sometimes I for-
    get and bend o-
        ver to sweep up

what once I could
    in one unthink-
        ing fluid move.

Or go to leap
    up after some-
        thing: and the thought

glows and fountains,
    something else free-
        zing the body,

gravity's side-
    kick holding me
        back, or spiting

my rise with dam-
    age. It is like
        phoning the num-

ber of someone
    who has moved a-
        way. Or like go-

ing to visit
    the house you were
        born in and (get-

ting it right – the
    town, the street, the
        lot – from heart, map-

less) coming on
    a gap, a rect-
        angle of white.

Cool Pastoral on Bloor Street

1. Consider the tragic fortitude
    of mannikins, the courage it takes
        under casual poses to do
    nothing interminably each day.

    To face unflinching (through sunlit glass
    that bars them from it) the rushing surf
        of life within reach where they must stand
    marooned on their islands' plastic turf,

    and not to cry out: more heroic
    than those Romans the lava rain stunned
        to statues – misshaped by the panic
    that twisted their limbs, glazed with their pain

    in black rock – friezes of agony.
    You would never know, from the relaxed
        swivel of this woman's wrist as she
    completes a backhand with her racket,

    that she will never take another
    swing, or from her smile that she has stood
        balanced here on one foot all summer
    like one of Dante's damned, and not cracked.

2. 'Cracked' is my father's word for 'crazy,'
    as in 'You'd have to be cracked to pay
        that much for a pair of shoes.' He's not
    crazy, but he forgets, and today

    as we pay out his visit's hours
    strolling on Bloor, he thinks up the same
        questions again minutes after he's
    nodded and smiled at answers to them.

Looking for things to look at and not
think, I focus on another grove
of mummers: headless, their necks poke out
like worms from the smartly turned-over

collars of turtlenecks and jackets.
You can tell they've also lost their arms
from the way the sleeves plummet slackly
off their shoulders – although they, ashamed

to show the mutilation, act cool
and tuck the cuffs into their pockets.
I look at my father – hands trembling,
head crazed like china with minute cracks

through which years exit invisibly –
and must remind myself his show is
kinder, the long-running comedy
where he's played every part, from fresh-faced

mooning lover to child-duped parent
to doddering senex: still free now
(while heart and limbs play their duet)
to do a walk-on, ad lib, bow out.

He sweats a little in the sunshine.
Summer stock, lacking the tragic poise
that freezes these actors in thcir sccnc,
we move on towards a shadier place.

The Finger Puppets in the Attic Dollhouse

If they, more petite
  than the mice whose flittings
    have pillaged their robes' sparkled trim,

stood tiptoe
  on the plumped felt tops
    of their thimble-sized footstools

to scrutinize
  the worn fabric
    of this room's blue distances,

would they locate
  the source of lightning bolts
    in our faces' wrinkled pleats

and construe the stars'
  dance from the tattered
    embroidery of our steps,

or find in our seamless
  unravelling years
    the tissue of apocalypse?

Dead Reckoning

We face each other down – me and this lock.
It teases me, turning cartwheels with my numbers
while my remembered turns fail me, clockwise
and counterclockwise. Dumb lock. *Yeah! Who's dumber!*

Starless navigator, I spin the wheel
and from deep plated nooks hear piston noises –
clicks and uncouplings fingers can just feel,
relentings – but the thing keeps its locked poise.

I need to bypass the ranks of rulebound housing
and match wits with the kingpin, one-on-one.
So I quit calculating and let my fingers
dance a blind reel, an eyepatched sailor's turn:

the lock's bright prow leaps out, flying home-free,
its combination still escaping me.

My Titanic

To see him hidden in a little skiff, whom but
a little before the whole Sea could not suffice
                (Robert Ashley, tr. *Loys le Roy*, 1594)

   Another phonecall, almost as bad
as the visit when you plied the dozen prints
   I'd brought. You flipped through once, twice – would
have gone on eagerly all afternoon,
   a small boat skipping over swell
upon smiling swell. Each wave, completely new,
   splashed you with fresh surprise: the pools
I watched you thrash in were jetstreams for you.
   Today, you sailed through six months in
a week, thinking you'd moved into 'this place'
   'some days' ago, your landmarks thinned
to mist, your clocks stopped: are you practising
   for death, or floating in a kind
of immortality? Time-study man
   out of time now, these wasteful rounds
defeat your skills and leave me, dead phone in
   my hand, mourning a presence less
substantial than a loss.
                    Time was when I
   rode on your shoulders through the walls
of looming breakers at Far Rockaway
   or Montauk, where the waves' green glass
bore down like translucent steamrollers
   shaking the earth, an arched menace
that collapsed inwards as it threatened us,
   then shattered into icy streams
tickling the toes sticking out where your
   braced hands battened around my feet.

You were my own Titanic, great wave strider,
    and when I grew too unwieldy
for shoulder passage, your pace set the pace
    along the ocean-sized thresholds
you led me through, outer and inner spaces
    where going lifted into flight –
Mount Washington, Ahab's whalehunt, Melchior's
    tenor cresting Rossini's heights
on LPs where I still feel every tremor
    though it's been decades.
                            Seven months
before your own launch, the Titanic's hull
    passed down its slipway. You lay berthed
safe in your mother's arms the night it sailed
    beneath our world. Now, finally,
you follow, as the staterooms of your mind
    fill with icewater, memories
panic and drown, the weight of what is blind
    and deaf and timeless pulls you down
to vacancy. And then? Another phonecall:
    an unfamiliar voice, a tone
of practised sorrow. Ropes lowering
    your narrow wooden skiff into
a denser element. Salvage, if ever,
    unthinkable.
                    Yet, I still think –
no matter how much salvaged proof of loss
    surfaces – of the ship intact,
a moon crossing black seas made brilliant by
    its own reflections. Ragtime tunes
float in the air where jewelled couples glide
    down the Grand Staircase, its inlays
untouched by woodworm. Stewards make their rounds
    parting the hours with dinner-bells,

while stokers belowdecks in boiler rooms
　　stir the undying fires. My need
for wholeness, largeness, harmony, propels
　　the heavenly body onward, freed
from mean necessity.
　　　　　　　　　As we still call
　　on the earth's moon for passage through
our nights, and feel it lift us with a power
　　something like love, the way it draws
the tides.
　　　　　　We, like the moon, beyond a core
　　of dust and reflected light, gifted
with insubstantial forces that become
　　our strongest ties. Now they lift me
over your head, clear through the warm, salt stream.

The Swing: A Valediction for My Daughter

This is some valediction: you're
airborne an ocean beyond hearing, and I'm
speechless, winding the clock in a living room
    as heavy with unsalvageable
    absence as an underwater
wreck. Yet the pendulum, as I haul

    up the weights that keep it swinging,
raises an image of you (long submerged
but polished to a sheen by the hushed current)
    and cradles it: you're two years old,
    we've lifted you from everything
you've ever known, and you won't be consoled.

    The sinking jet, the bare, loud flat
in England must have drawn you, kicking, back
through your birth-plunge, when you dived into waking,
    and noise first broke into your ears,
    and breath broke from your lips and left
worse noise. Out walking, cradling you, your fears,

    our guilt, we set you on a swing:
slowly, from your sailing yellow rainhood,
you sighted peace, your hands hugging the chains
    that kept you on your course. You hauled
    us to that distant park (*'m' along!*)
day after day because the pendulum

    you rode, tucked in your leather sling,
only looked like it was going nowhere,
but took you on a course of circular
    homecoming, to the safe harbour
    of your first cruise – a berthed floating
towards seaworthiness, dreamily provisioning.

Or did that swing bring comfort by
playing out, through its pulsing sway, the strokes
of the long-distance swimmer in the hold
    of your own ribcage? Cradled in
    an image of its kick-and-glide,
you pushed ahead, not back, into the green

    branches swaying in the wind
over the land you're flying towards right now.
The heart, like a pendulum, stroking through
    what looks like anchored coming-back,
    surges forward in new rounds,
free because it navigates a wakeless

    and unpredictable expanse.
Its escapement won't allow retreat
up along the chain of unreeled hours
    into the spool that, wound-up, once
    held them – and you. Fly on, sweet heart
over the rooted trees, and make your home

    in motion, like the swing, knowing
that every landing is a port of call
and not a settlement. May the heavy pull
    of parting carry you along
    to find again the source of true
peace in a moving swing: you have it in you.

Heartstrings

in old notions of Anatomy, the tendons
or nerves supposed to brace and sustain
the heart (OED)

1. We know that no such things exist. The heart,
   in our books, shows up without strings attached –
   pure flexing muscle, quite able to stand
   up for itself.
                 Yet, in the margin of
   the field behind our house one afternoon,
   I could make out the source of those old notions.
   A rabbit – no taut muscles quivering
   as when they crouch – lay basking on the earth.
   Only its misted eyes shrank back from death,
   its body shamelessly relaxed, even
   the one long slit, throat to genitals,
   a bloodless opening like the lapels
   of a fur coat stretched wide for the sun's warmth.
   Inside the slit, complicated beauty
   dazzled, the rabbit's treasure chest on show:
   over a maze of crescents at the base,
   light and dark in love, organ and organ
   side by side; at the higher end,
   the trachea's shaft descending from the head
   intact, a fluted alabaster aisle
   where air once glided down towards hidden rooms
   to change to living breath – vacated now;
   and, at the centre, nestled behind a shield
   of bone, that dark mass had to be the heart –
   or was the one beside it? Which parts were
   the vessels, in that web of tubes and membranes,
   and which the thing itself? Although dead still,
   the tubes swerved and blurred, a ball of roots
   too interlaced to tease apart by looking:
   nothing there but themselves to 'brace and sustain' –
   a heart all strings.

                    The kind of heart I felt
inside, as I intruded on this creature
no larger than a baby, that had paid for
my access to its beauty with its life:
my heart no muscle, but a helpless knot
of strings pulled on, tautness stretched into pain.

2. Isn't that how you learn to feel your heart?
   It ties part of itself around something
   outside of you – a comforter, a toy –
   which lets you know how far away you are
   by tugging on the string: a distance-gauge
   that renders space as pain. You grow: your heart
   makes more attachments, and its mesh of strings
   ravels and reaches to so many pegs
   that sometimes you can hardly move without
   convulsing the whole rigging, every turn
   recoiling through the strings in pain.
                                        Or joy,
   even when laced with pain, that distance can
   be bridged invisibly, your racing heart
   keeping you one with what appeared to be
   apart – a joy you met with as a child
   when you made 'telephones' of two tin cans
   by linking them (lidless, scrubbed back to their
   unlabeled, fresh-pressed gleam) with string, passed through
   a small hole punched in each flat end, then knotted
   to keep from slipping out. When you cupped
   the open end of one can to your ear,
   a sea-shell murmur suddenly gave way
   to throat vibrations: you could hear the voice
   (could feel it too) of someone far down the street,
   two children linked by string. The longer the string,
   the more you held onto a miracle;
   the more you pulled it taut, the clearer the sound.

3. Heartstrings carry music, not just sound.
   When I lie with my ear close to your heart,
   the gentle breathing moving through your lungs
   must play across your heartstrings as across
   a wind-harp, since my heartstrings move with yours
   in harmony (it quivers through my blood)
   and to make harmony you need music –
   a reach beyond mere sound.
                                    A stretch of music
   nothing like the 'harmony of the spheres'
   you learn of in old books: this joyful noise
   is human, not celestial, and won't
   play on forever, but the instrument
   is strong enough to brace us and sustain us,
   the music sweet enough to feel it heaven
   to hang on every breath, listening for more.

TWO

Touching in Detail: A Glosa for Elizabeth Bishop

I never knew him. We both knew this place,
apparently, this literal small backwater,
looked at it long enough to memorize it,
our years apart. How strange. And it's still loved.

('Poem')

I never knew *you*, never even met you
(although – who knows – we might have shared the same
subway car once in Brooklyn, strangers: you
paying a visit to Miss Moore, and me
a kid riding home from a visit to the zoo,
both of us going to sleep that night graced
with visions of exotic animals),
but when I think of you, the sight of *him*
comes into mind. Although I see his face,
I never knew him. We both knew this place

and loved it – he, because he'd spent his childhood
running among the trees in the old orchard
(ramshackle even then, worm-eaten apples
dropping forgottenly into the tall grass)
and I, because I'd never known such peace,
lulled in my cradle by the ceaseless clatter
of wheels along the elevated tracks
running outside the living-room window
of our walkup third-floor cold-water flat.
Apparently, this literal small backwater

(its well tapping a spring that fed a nameless
rill that itself flowed to the widely unknown
Coates Creek) gave us sufficient common ground
to raise a rare grin on his taciturn
face – you would know its like from your childhood
in Nova Scotia: poor soil to grow smiles in –
the night he first walked me around the fencelines
and I picked up one of the worthless windfalls
and polished it. He, seeing I prized it,
looked at it long enough to memorize it

and, through the grin that broke out, said 'I must
have picked a great grandparent of that apple
when you were far-off as a speck of dust
up there among the stars.' Yet, that detail
brought us together: it was where we touched,
although we met just once before he moved
away. And you? I see him when I think of you
because your art is also a prized windfall
you – dust now, exotic – touch me through, over
our years apart. How strange. And it's still loved.

Sirens

The sirens sang through my first years –
　　not the Wagnerian
twilight of air-raids and all-clears
　　with deadly percussion,

but a postwar wailing in small towns
　　tunnelling through night air
to bring the walls of sleep down on
　　dream's sheeted furniture.

Somewhere a door slammed shut, a car's
　　muffled salvo started,
and the town's wakened volunteers
　　moved against fire with water.

By daylight, from my post upstairs
　　I watched the black smoketrail
spiral like a downed bomber,
　　then raise a white gauze flag

and thin to nothing or waves of heat
　　where the all-clear floated.
Some winter days, air heavy with
　　the thick white downward smoke

of snow carried the all-clear's call
　　when there had been no fire:
after a nightlong siege, the school
　　was signalling surrender.

I built my ally snow a fort
　　with a snow sentinel
on guard all day – but overnight
　　the west wind swept the clouds'

tattered resistance from the sky,
   driving them to foothills
along its southeast rim. Daybreak
   saw cold march through the silence

of its own merciless all-clear,
   turn my snowman to stone,
and rake tongues of unbroken fire
   across east window panes

which struck their colours in an hour
   but held, that long school day,
lost freedom's frozen tracks – or ghosts
   of the sirens' soundwaves.

Tarpaper

1. Look to the moon, they always said, or listen
    for the creek's unwaning spill of crescendo
        to fill your eyes and ears
    in place of green leaves and the cricket's plainsong;
        they will sustain you through the year's
    declining light and heat, and your own.

    But the creek's words stick frozen in its throat;
        cold has stopped the wind's tin whistle;
            and the moon's no help: its round
    idiot face takes in the snow and floats
        trapped where, rivalling hardened ground,
    the wash of stars has set to dark blue marble.

2. I have walked out tonight – called from my warm
    kitchen by black on the horizon,
        deeper than the streaked shoals
    of sky that border it – to where the farm
        ends at half-buried, iced split rails.
    Moonlight spills through them, shimmer of white neon,

    but I can't take my eyes off that black well
        which, closer now, resolves into
            the north wall of a house –
    derelict once, bought, half brought back from rubble
        by a handyman's devotion
    whose soft slowness thwarts what his hands do.

3. Last year he picked its withered crop of shingles,
        and on the bared, waterstained wood
            he tacked up tarpaper
    in sheets, like sketching-paper on an easel
        propped behind a stack of cedar
    he meant to face it with before the cold

set in. The stack, now taller by two feet
   of drift, matches corded hardwood
      heaped against the side
he did finish – a pale wall out of sight
   from here, where one coal-black facade
must stand for the whole house asleep behind it.

4. It is enough: although all fall its rawness
      pained like an unbandaged wound,
         tonight the wall prevails
   against an enemy that has slung chains
      from eaves and porch, and turned handrails
   to glistening treachery. Alone it stands,

   black woodstove warming up the earth's cold kitchen
      with its soft, perishable skin
         of tar – preservative
   whose power comes from its decomposition –
      in the inhuman dead of winter
   standing for what's unfinished and alive.

Cora's Quilts

If I could lift her from the parlor where
    her quilting frame stands propped
at the room's centre like a tipped garden,
    lift her in her aproned
housedress and coarse support stockings – without

the travel documents and Sunday clothes
    that, more than any flight,
might distance who she is and what she knows –
    and set her down in front
of the great tapestry that ran unbroken

through the old Bishop's Palace at Bayeux,
    she would be more taken
by scenes embroidered on the cloth's borders
    than the spurred panoply
rolling along its high road to glory.

Those smaller people, not so richly threaded,
    tell the kind of story
she knows, where hands wield spades or forks, not sceptres,
    and hunched shoulders worry
ploughshares through mean acreage, under skies

unfavoured with the weavings of falcons.
    Sharpened by loss, her eyes
would scan the laid-and-couched wool's chainmailed ranks
    the way shears glance through gauze;
would trace the spear – strayed from the main design –

that takes a wide-mouthed labourer aback,
    and recognize the pain
of someone marginal caught in the wreck
    of a vast, wayward machine.
She would feel closest kinship with the hand

that wove the hem's more parabolic scenes –
   vague meadow or woodland
visited by fabled amphisbaena,
   griffon, and other winged
horrors – not from downhome fascination

with chintz grotesques, trapunto bric-a-brac,
   but in grim concession
to the oblique approach the hand must make
   towards what the heart would shun:
terror or pain too large for any template.

Nothing to do but cut squares, triangles –
   shapes free of love or hate –
and line them up like holographic figures
   that pulse through double takes
to almost-catch the near-miss of each light.

So, in her Dutch Rose quilt, shot satin whorls
   glance in metal-glitter
towards silver spurs, or stars, or the disc harrow
   a groundhog hole took in
and elbowed over, thirty-five years back,

to pin her son Fred underneath a tractor
   ('young Fred,' who 'grew up quick'
and was at fourteen taller than his father).
   Who knows if those puckered
backstitches feathering from the spinning flowers

are wisps of weed, or heat waves rising from
   an engine powering
useless, upended wheels? Her quilting frame
   now bears, in tight-knit rows,
a field of battle, now a farmer's field

where something spills out or is harvested.
   Its most unearthly yield
takes you light years from Bayeux's rust-wooled canvas:
   all blues, the pattern called
Shadow Star. Look where tapered, cobalt-blue bars

target and nearly obliterate small azure
   planets, a cosmic war
the dark side wins. Look twice – the shafts form rays
   of light, the planets their stars:
a pulse to comfort weaker eyes than hers.

Mel's Barn

In memory of F. Melville Caswell, 1913–1996

God must have lived there – heaven knows
it was too big to be a human house:
so high it brewed its own weather of mists
and captive rainbows up around the roofbeams,
where light hung polished from the fissures
in an arsenal of spare thunderbolts.

Outside, its timbered walls lorded
like sheer grey rock over the lesser hills
of neighbouring farms, even when the light
of aging winter afternoons softened
the roof peak's iceblade, sheathing slopes
of burnished snow in watery deep blue.

In winter storms it was less ark
than harbour, a fixed anchorage when squalls
sank the horizon and raked fields shifted
their whitecapped tides. Cold sucked Mel's chimney smoke
up a thin siphon, but the barn
would hold its breath and stay under for weeks.

Mel was the barn's man: he belonged
to it. He oiled the great barred jaw's hinges
and swept up scraps from heaped wagons that shivered
over the ramp's threshold, load after load
into the insatiable gloom.
He stacked its ribbed galleries with blond fuel,

and in return the barn killed Mel
by inches. As he aged, it gathered all
the years of dead weights he had lifted, heaved
its giant mass behind them and bore down
in fury on his joints. It breathed
fumes of ripe silage over him; quickened,

old threshing dust arose in clouds
and ate like locusts through the reddening
fields of his lungs. It fastened on his heart
failing wingbeats left among the rafters
by generations of trapped birds
whose flights south ended in its leafless wood.

Nothing the barn could do weakened
Mel's love for what it held and what it gave.
It held the wind's tide, dry as running grain,
bodying him and piping through the eaves
until their vents became his ears –
his thoughts drawn into sound, his mind grown choir.

The barn gave what his eyes took in
whenever he climbed its back and found again
a tiered world waiting there, brimming around him
as bright as if the sun had poured the hills
minutes before and they, all shimmer,
hung fire, too filled with being to be still.

Acolyte in bibbed overalls,
what could he do, the night a spear of light
pierced the barn's head and brought it down in flames,
but stare at nothing over the charred wood –
too loyal to defect to blind
chance, and too old to raise another god.

This Green Plot Shall Be Our Stage

1. Lincoln Cathedral, 1244

'Exterminate these altogether,' rules
  the Bishop. He deplores how 'plays' –
  harvest rites, tinselled 'miracles' –
invade the very bulwarks of the soul.

Lead-helmeted, stone-armoured, wooden-ribbed
  churches, reared to be God's soldiers,
  fall to Satan, leaving exposed
earthworks, mere flesh and blood. Open lips –

prayer's threshold once – serve as the porch from which
  shadows take flight. His Grace believes
  only one actor's soul survived
such seizure: when Our Lord, His body bleached

to light, rendered the sun; until the day
  that sun rises again, man's role
  is the unnamed, nearly wordless
servant who holds the torch. Only one play

other than Scripture's two-act mystery
  pleases His Grace – that of natural
  light on the glass and stone hatches
of this ark, landed on a promontory

above the shoals of Lincolnshire: the waves
  of figures on the west face grow
  solid with sunset, as when cold
morning air bodies breath. He will not live

to see the transept window whose design
  preserves his gaze: the Bishop's Eye –
  stone pupil, night-blind, irised by
a ring of fall leaves set in lead and iron.

2. *Plum Creek Farm, 1990*

The children need the dark to start their play.
   Once we've moored two campstools in
   a shallow of the wrinkled lawn's
drift, where their sandbox anchored once, we wait

behind the bramble patch: pick and nibble
   a few last berries, try to look
   like we're not trying to look back
at the tree, nautical in spotlight-rigging,

whose mainmast forms their set. It founders now:
   old hulk, listing with rusted apples,
   sinking into its shadow-cape
like us, dwarfed by our own lengthening shadows.

A middle-aged Adam and Eve who have
   years of lost gardens to look back on,
   we would shelter growing children
from knowing that the lawn's sunset-capped waves

give no more lasting footing than water.
   But now they call us to our seats:
   the usher takes our leaf-tickets,
the stagehands link up wires – one ornaments

the cricket's solo with taped violins,
   one overlays the tree's scarred trunk
   with green and yellow sequins. Soon,
our hammock holds sleep-tricked Titania,

and Oberon, waving a wand of ripe clover,
   gets caught red-handed by a spill
   of light along Puck's taut rope slide.
Three imps: made up, costumed, and yet never

more free to be themselves, like folded moths
   unfurled by night – winged by the same
   'let's say' that raised the anchor chain
on sandbox expeditions. Then, their 'boat'

sailed off on waters rising from the same
   wellspring, within them, broken out
   to be the wave whose back they rode:
the thin but buoyant skin of sheer becoming.

They knew then what their bodies tell us now
   (grown into these new characters
   from shapes thrown off like Act One's cape) –
there's no still life. We sleepwalk through a show

of moving stages, shifting sets, and find
   ourselves here in a shadowed tree's
   quick changes, metamorphoses
seen best at nightfall, when the sun's blindfold

can't hide the scaffolding of air behind
   the most bricklike of brick facades.
   Sensing in our thickened bodies
a like transparency (with such breaths as wind

lends to a sail) we, in this buoyant glow,
   awake to freedom, paradise
   regained: the power of child's play
to know the hard world's core as a dream-flow.

3. Stratford-upon-Avon, 1995

Outside this afternoon, the river hefts
   not only its accustomed weight
   of swans, canoes, and houseboats, but
a whole flotilla of launched trees, cloud-rafts,

and brick outriggers crammed with cars; even
   the theatre rests on watered silk
   a footfall would unweave. These tricks
of light are child's play to the mage within.

He's conjured up storm, shipwreck, resurrection,
   and clothed high spirits in the robes
   of gods; but he knows no fable
can save the globe – either the little one

we orbit, moon-faced, in the theatre's night,
   or the great globe spinning beneath,
   that sharpens first, then rubs us smooth,
then wears us down to dust. 'Every third thought'

will be his grave – and yet his comedy
   comes round to freedom and return,
   as if he'd rummaged in the earth's
dark hold and found a sun, and ridden it,

the way these children once rode their sandbox.
   They sit beside us, sharing his
   sandy shore in the dark, their eyes
led by his spell beyond the stage business

to half-see what their ears take in as music:
  those shapes that breath carves in the air,
  a flowing architecture more
divine than stained glass fixed in stone, because

pure spirit – volatile, untouchable
  essence of life. As this man well
  knew when he gave his Ariel
up to the elements, and left a world of verbs

islanded on air. He bound no play
  in print, because he saw through ink's
  blind worship of earth's solid lines.
He knew 'Let there be light' lives in 'let's say.'

Flights

Medieval hammers staked claims to the
    otherworldly
  when prayer, quarried from thatched
hovels, rose stone by stone into
    gothic arches.

They never would have thought it up:
    Victorians, steeped
  in heaviness, who sank
this farmhouse like a brick spade
    in the hill's flank.

It took a city boy, kite-flyer
    through deep defiles
  of concrete, to surprise
the updraft hidden in the steps'
    tight-lidded rise

and ride it lightward in an act
    of faith, a kite
  of air stretched on the lattice
the window-crossbar's shadow held
    for the sun to hoist.

He ripped out the back stairs and opened
    a lighter way upward,
  trading hardwood risers
for the unearthly buoyancy
    of treading water:

light pooled in that uncovered well.
    The papered wall
  beside the window fluttered
where enthralled water-birds rose on
    translucent feathers.

When he needed wider light
    for herds to graze,
  he moved on over the hill,
where skies, let out to the horizon,
    trailed long white tails.

Living in the old house, we varied
    his ways and lowered
  flowerpots from pulleys
on the ceiling, buckets brimming
    over his well.

On winter nights, wings rose in waves
    from our cookstove
  at the well's base: a source
we could believe in, a pulse far
    from the cold stars –

flight that left no stone monument
    but lightly spent
  all its life in flashes,
as flame, breaking free, demolished
    arches of ash.

The Sharpness of the Eye:
A Tribute to Samuel van Hoogstraten

The last angels were packing up
To leave even the margins of the world.
A few still lurked amid the shrubbery
   Glimpsed through the Gothic-arched window
Of a room where a virgin hugged her baby
   Or some saint expired; one or two

Boldly showed up as large as life,
Their velvet robes lapping the plain tiled floor
Where the girl knelt to hear she was God's wife,
   But you sensed the awkward, painful
Challenge of their encumbered, thin-winged flight,
   And were glad they kept it from you.

They'd grown too weighty for their wings:
Only cherubs vaulted like tennis balls
Between cloud puffs high over the manger,
   And even they dared not dawdle
(Having lost the hummingbird hang of it)
   For lute or clarion solos.

You can see them at Bath Abbey,
Refugees on the Late Gothic facade.
Some, with angelic patience, pick their way
   Up the tall rungs, bulky brocades
Bunched and raised in their free hands, prudently;
   Some wait below with suitcases.

They'd cleared out of the Low Countries
Before his birth, perhaps because flat land
Promised – unlike the Alps or Pyrenees –
   No great relief for the earthbound.
What's certain is that his first canvases
   Supplanted haloed arrangements

With bare-headed mortals brooding
From dark-beamed rooms over stone windowsills,
Facing us, outfacing the gloom brewing
  Behind their backs. What's different from
His master Rembrandt's encrusted brushwork
  Is the sharp slit between the lips

In his self-portrait, as if speech
Hovered there in mid-flight between the life
Behind the canvas and the life reaching
  To meet it, and as if a knife
And not a brush had outlined an approach
  To secular infinity:

No cloud-capped arches, but a sluice
As flat as Holland's rivers, like them lithe
And navigable, time carrying us
  Along a current, endless path
Whose course resurfaces with each fresh glance.
  That slit anticipates the depths

The flat walls of his masterpiece
Summon us to explore: 'Perspective Box,'
So like a dollhouse it could be dismissed
  As nothing more than childish tricks,
A sideshow juggling with our sense of space
  To tease us into long vistas

Of pigment. Think of it, instead,
As his Annunciation, witness to
The mystery of a transfigured world
  Laid open by the insistence
Of an interrogating eye: the boards
  Of our homemade, mortal houses,

No longer brushed by angels' wings,
Were more than coffin-wood to box us in;
They could be doorways giving onto ranged
   Interiors, elevations
Of unlimited room. The eye could bring
   Depths to light, by sighting its own

   Disclosures in the restless play
Of an unstable world where even stone
Will not stay stone. So he sharpened his eye –
   For 'any part of nature can
Whet its sharpness' – on this shuttered hallway,
   And made light of our density.

Turner's Eye

A perfect storm.

The sea thrashes its tail, agony
rides the bucking train
        of its flailed, hanging flesh and exposed bone:
plummets, crashes, recoils

        only there are ten thousand tails,
heaving and plunging over and under each other
        to weave out of the agony
a knotted oneness, a pulsating brocade

        only it is hard and jagged, rocky, a range
of peaks and crags broken from their foundations,
        surges of rolling granite, a whole
stone landscape on the boil

        only no lava simmers, no red rocks
melt in this sub-zero swell
        far below the most cold-
blooded pulse of animal heat:

        ice-irised at its
core, the black glass of Medusa's
        pupil freezes
all.

                * * *

He had the sailors lash him
to the *Ariel*'s mast: four hours in the storm
shadowing Ulysses, sharing Ulysses' hunch
that power over the waves' madness
lay with the ear – that the sea's mane of snakes
(slapping timbers, slithering through the rigging)
moved to a music. He opened his ears:
runs of wind and water flowed into
his head. He trapped them there,

conjured them, made them flow
onto the canvas, knowing that motion –
passing the eye, *at* but never *into* –
was always the ear's to experience. So we hear
the storm's roar calling through the pigment,
we feel it rumble through the great framed sail,
Snow Storm: Steamboat off a Harbour's Mouth.
It is this pitch of vertigo – this
sea-shell tipping of the ear, enthralled
to free the eye from its fixed gaze –
that heaves us into the swoop of wave and wind
and makes us gods.

* * *

This, the superhuman view:
to float free of the heavy onlyness
            of place, to be
on the ship you look at from a distance.

No storm can daunt us, there is nothing
out there can touch us, there is
            nothing out there:
only what we make by looking.

What powers the boat is not
the patch of white that hovers half
            before, half behind the mast,
a ghostly sheeting of reflected light,

            but the black wheel below, pupil
and mill. Its glower churns
            the waves we ride, lashes and welts
the air with chains of spray, rakes salt shrapnel

            through the snow's flapping scrim. (All
show. Lower the curtain,
            close the eye
and it goes

                away: every
blink
        a little
apocalypse.)

                * * *

Drivewheel, onyx eye,
one with those slopes
no foot will ever print,
one with the un-
embraceable snow:
we feel your pull,
the black ice of your sluice.
Yours is the whirlpool's kiss
in which we cannot breathe.
In your perfect circle,
tearless, undistorted,
only the wind
has breath, only
the waves' hollows
well with salt water.
Crystal-filmed, peerless shell,
only the eye of death
can take all in –
'the imagination of the artist
enthroned in his own recess,
incomprehensible
as the cause of darkness.'
God and cipher,
disembodied sailor,
life is the harbour's mouth
you will never reach,
love (hovering in the sheeting,
an imperfect patch of white)
the Penelope you will never know.

The Glass Flowers *

1.

It's human to burn
                    to be more than human –
to torch our way out of the iron frame.

Breath fans the runner's hope
                              that somewhere
in the next lap
                with one stride
                                his inner runner
will leave
          the burnt-out body
                              to become
                                        pure phantom speed.

The ballerina's fire
                     transfigures
the stepped fountain
                     of her spiral
from foam
          through mist
                       into the spirit of mist.

Or, if we can't
                turn into
wisp or shimmer
                we turn our hands

* Harvard University's collection of glass flowers, developed to teach
  botany, was created between 1887 and 1936 by Leopold and Rudolf
  Blaschka at their studio near Dresden, Germany. The collection's 3000
  models of over 830 species of plants are among world's most exquisite
  works in glass. Dresden was destroyed by Allied bombing on Fasching
  (Feb. 13, 1945), the traditional mardi gras night before Ash Wednesday.

to intricate mimicry
                of nature's
                        distillations.

Two lampworkers
                father and son
                        'passionately fond of glass'
flamed
      its sheer
              ice
to molten scree
            and then
coaxed
      flowers
            from the cooldown's
shards.

With simple tweezers
              files
needles
     their hands
transformed the revenants of sand's holocaust
                        into garden gods.

Here irises' blue-watered silks
                  ripple without wind
nepenthes' tendrils thread around
                    spools of moonlight
the prickly pear
            spreads petal-fans more spectral
than the scrim of tulle
        a thinning wave
                slips over the sand.
                          All elemental sand
fired clear, the glass
         flowers.

2.

No, it only seems to. Blow all day
  at those pollen-laden strands of goldenrod
and not one grain of powder drifts away.
  Lean your hand on the display case where

aquatic popweed floats on waterless tides
  of windowlight: submerged leaf-filaments
(tiny and blanched as root hairs) start to quiver –
  but in death's dance, driven along senseless

on the wake of your pulse. The lily buds' sealed-up
  chrysalids will be their funeral urns,
and maple nurslings in the folds of sleep
  are mummies suckled on formaldehyde.

Here 'the most wonderful plant in the world' (Darwin
  on the Venus flytrap) starves with unworldly
patience, its bird-beak leaves locked open wide
  for wingless, bodiless eternity.

3.

Father and son, death's two naïve
accomplices. What would they do
if you could bring them back to see
evolution's most artful flowers

fail? Not just those small betrayals
of matter, where the fleshy coat
has peeled from its bare bone of glass,
or the purely symbolic defeat

of blossoms laid out in a box
for safekeeping, then sent on show
by cushioned hearse. No, the big tricks
of history. Their Germanic passion

for a glass free of impurities –
for perfect specimens in bloom
a thousand years – grown virulent;
the furnace that refined their dreams

metastasized to a hell-mouth
that ate six million intricate,
unique lives; and, in turn, their whole
city become a furnace, its

updraft fanning storms of flame
to wither wrought iron foliage,
its sparks seeding an eight-day rain,
bits of dead children's mardi gras

costumes like petals floating down
on the razed garden. Would they turn –
that childless couple, father and son –
to art to give body to their pain?

Would they extrude a perfect tear
of lead crystal – all polished void
with a stillbirth's heft? Or would their hearts,
broken away from designing hands,

burning out of control, force
artless water from their eyes?

    water that – like the perpetual ice
    of glass – cannot put out the fire

        shimmer that – like us – comes and goes
        and can give life only to dying flowers.

THREE

Hummingbird

'Where do passions
    find room in so
        diminutive
            a body?' asks
Hector St. John
    de Crèvecoeur in
        Letters from an
            American
Farmer, shocked by
    a finger-long
        power bobbin's
            hot current: wings
spinning themselves
    invisible,
        a needle-mouth
            siphoning half
the body's weight
    each day, a heart's
        thousand stitches
            per minute, and
(most distressing)
    the petit point
        that leaves a limp
            red-threaded bag
where there was once
    a rival bird.
        Passions find room
            by purging the
hummingbird of
    everything not
        passion: no song;
            no orifice
to smell the bloom
    it plunders; legs
        mere filaments.
            Yet, a songbird

might sacrifice
        size, leisure, peace
            for a brief life
                whose song is flight,
whose heart converts
        sugar to speed
            spinning, spinning
                the sun's gold thread.

A World of Light

If I close my eyes now, I can still see them
canopied by the visor of my sunhat:
three children islanded on a narrow rim
of earth between the huge crack-willow that
they squat before, hushed, poised to net a frog,
and the pond the frog will jump to (it got away)
a glass its dive will shatter.
                            The unbroken image
pleases my mind's eye with its density,
such thick crisscross of tree-trunk, earth, and tall grass
I see no breach, no source for the light that steeps it
but a blue burning in the pond's green glass.

The grass withered, the tree blew down, earth caught
the frog, the children grew. Sky's ice-blue flame
teased along the wick it would consume.

Clark Kent Leaves His Clothes at Midland

'Look! Up in the sky!
It's a bird – it's a plane – it's ...'
– but what about, I used to wonder,
the people who were looking down
and found, in all those phonebooths,
the piles of crumpled clothes:
shined shoes, shining trousers,
white shirt (ball-point, datebook
left in the pocket), and on top of all,
tossed off like a signature,
the window-glass hornrims.
Did they get used to it?
Pick them up, pack them off
c.o.d. c/o *The Daily Planet?*
Or did they cut them up
and pass them out like relics – moultings
of the flown spirit?
                    Yet, who would
want bits of Clark Kent? Men of steel
are precious, but Clark Kent's
flesh was soft, sharing our itch
to peel the spirit's husk, tearing
into phonebooths, saunas, bedrooms
or other sweaty confessionals
to shuck the trappings of the daily mess
and let the cramped soul free.

                    * * *

In Midland, at the centre
of the Huron Indian Village,
a primitive low booth:
bonepit of the Wendat, keeper
of the spirits of creatures
that nourished the fled tribe.
A humble shrine, no higher
than a water stoup – but dry,

the bones curing to driftwood shards
or splinters of barnboard.
Time has smoked them out
until they match the ribbed stockade's
bleached cedar. Nuggets
of drumstick, wingbones,
a walnut-small clavicle: when poked,
they click like softwood slats.
Full-toothed, a feral jawbone
hangs, with no more bite
than a broken clothespeg.
                              Was this
the elders' intention? A jigsaw
lesson, pieced out in driest wise:
that bones are nothing special,
trappings left behind
when the captive flares its cape
and takes off; that the glimmer
behind the horny socket
comes from another planet
and is happiest airborne.

                    * * *

   Cooped up in a new world
of bare planed board, thick cloth,
tin candlesticks and mugs, Brébeuf
must have been struck by the delicate
intricacy, the lacelike overlappings
that flute and furl the ivory surface
on candle drippings like this, my souvenir
filched from his restored mission
at Sainte-Marie Among the Hurons.
As he sat writing by the source
of similar wax cascades, perhaps
their shimmer of channelling threads
put him in mind of old world fountains

or foaming cathedral pinnacles
where stone, shedding its heaviness,
feathers and flares.
                    But did he see,
before the Iroquois flames
rendered his flesh as clear
as molten candle wax,
that wax collapses
into these elaborate
bony exfoliations only
when the flame's wing shakes it off,
that the unfurling soul
flutters against
wick, black robe, bonepit,
too hot to hold
when most itself?

The sun's untouchable red cape,
up in the sky's sheer otherness.

Glen Huron

Heard filtered through the local dialect
at the local market
by ears that had to hear it twice
and still would not believe what they picked out:

Glen Urine? No place could be that despised
even though all the maps
overlooked it, if it gave rise
to baskets of such glass-bright early apples.

After I saw the place, I heard it more
as Glen Yearn, valley steeped
in longing of the Highland Scots
who settled where their homesickness could ripen

with McIntosh and Early Blaze – a fever
the Mad River fed
each spring, throwing off the winter
blanket, a racing pulse eroding orchards

until they calmed its foaming stream into
the broad lucidity
of a millpond. It still mutters
in corners where the woods bend down to listen,

and in October it ripples with their fever –
an older, homegrown grief.
Then, when cold water bears the leaves'
falling torches, Glen Yearn's valley reflects

a parting Huron's last look at his lost
Eden's uncut pines.
It flows with sunset-coloured waste
purged from the blood, relinquished and so despised.

Threads

Waman Puma dramatized the clash of cultures by having each man speak in his own tongue: *'Kay qoritachu mikhunki?'* asks the Inca. 'Do you eat this gold?' And the European answers yes, *'Este oro comemos!'* 'We eat this gold!'

(Ronald Wright,
Stolen Continents: The 'New World' Through Indian Eyes)

1. Imagine funny men
                    who go mountain climbing on horseback
            to discover a country known for thousands of years.

Who willingly bind their bodies
                    in tiny chains
            to bring
                    the iron age to cities in the sky.

Funny men with faces
                    woollier than mountain goats
        flesh
                    under the iron
                        white as maggots

who make love
                    with song and torch
            to the dead night
                            and close
                                    their eyes to the gifts
                                        of the rising sun.

2. Think of scraping the paint
                    off a Rembrandt
            to make a nice canvas mat

                    or erasing Shakespeare
                            for some clean white paper.
        Funny enough.

Now imagine melting
          a culture
merely to get
          lumps of raw metal.
               To eat.

Unimaginable.

3. They did not eat gold
                    they ate people
               iron teeth through flesh
                         armed only in wool

     courtyard slaughterhouses
          stacked with human meat

     blood like water
               finding its own level
          staining along runnels
                    carved for sacred springs.

     Those the white men couldn't
               stomach themselves
          they sent their germs
                    to season for the mouths of vermin.

          How can you see through eyes
                         pecked out?

4. Imagine a world spun from wool
               anchored
                    to granite mountains
                         whose fabric
                              mist questions

by cloudfleece
interwoven
with the maguey's fibre
braided into bridges

and under those wispy
cataracts
quicksilver rivulets threading
often invisibly
the nap of valleys

whose harvests are also threads
woven of nightshade
(how can the night tell shade?)

loveapple vines twining in sunlight
all but the red fruit deadly
tuberous nightshade worming black earth
each bulb a core of cloud-silk
tree tobacco's fatal azure bloom
blueprinting the smoked leaves' visionary fum

all insinuating the nothing at the heart of all
the all at the heart of nothing.

A world woven of cloudthread.

5. Shod and visored in iron
climbing up from the Inquisition's hell-mouth
they overlooked it all.

Bibles in hand
Hernando De Soto
Ponce de León
walked along tableland where seasons
never altered

through blossoms perpetually keeping perpetual promises
and kept on searching for Eden
walked among natives who
knew nothing of money
lacked all sense
of possession
and measured time in circles where
balanced at noon
on pillars of stone
spun light
from spools of sun
unwound liquidly
spilling no shadow

walked visored looking for the Golden Age.

6. They missed altogether the finest thread
the quipu
knotted thread tied in long fringes
nothing much to look at
something to listen to:

thread of the Inca chronicler's narrative
rope-bridge of the mind
spanner of storied chasms

memory's hand-hold
through the thin air
of an oral culture's slopes

yet no more a second-string stand-in
for an alphabet's fixed lines
than the sure-footed draft llama
a wagon lacking wheels

the quipu
    like the llama
        a live means of transport
            for threading living landscapes:

history no solid ground
    but shifting terrain
        somewhat shaken
    by the thundering speech of earthquakes

        and completely reshaped
            by the human mouth
                in the loom of telling.

7. Mountain winds whisper
    the names of Incas
        eaten by time:
    Huayna Capac
    Huascar
        Atahuallpa.

In mountain passes
    the wild nightshade
        flowering angel's-trumpet
        blows whiteness.

Through vacant lots
    over the conquered continents
        gold-tipped needles
            the anthers
                of common nightshade vines
            thread the wasted cities' rubble
                their stitching
            invisible
                under brick and concrete mountains
    telling
        not stories

but beads:
               the green-fruits-turning-red
                              of
        (native name unknown)
                       solanum dulcamara

'nightshade sweet-bitter'
        the taste
                and aftertaste
        of a paradise lost

rendered 'bittersweet'
        on the tongue
                of Elizabethan herbalist Gerard
        giving history
                        a sweet ending:

        'the juyce is good for those that have fallen
                from high places
                        for it is thought to dissolve
                blood congealed
                        and to heal
                                the hurt places.'

A National Dream

1. In hills too liquid to sit still,
   two trappers paddle across a lake,

   birchbark canoe and buckskin vests
   absorbed by mist, disembodied

   but for the red scarf in the bow,
   the blue scarf partner keeping pace,

   their quiet dip and rise miming
   waves over the quiet waves.

2. So for some years. One morning
   the red scarf cannot leave the tent

   where the canoe sleeps. From his knife
   the wake of one long cut severs

   bow from stern, the cradled bow
   as on a wave borne from the tent

   by blue scarf to the knife-edge where
   water's mirror doubles all

3. in mere illusion. He climbs in,
   paddles the bow across the lake,

   his dip and rise mimed by red scarf
   who, in the tent, paddles the stern

   through thoughts too liquid to sit still,
   dissolving distance between bow

   and stern, absorbed, both afloat
   on quiet waves over the waves.

The Crying Totem

a little old lady on the edge of nowhere – Emily Carr

Think of it as a mortuary pole,
   its face the crest of someone dead
   whose body, weathered light as bleached
cedar, is couched in the dugout of its head.

* * *

She crouches by the beached dinghy, squinting
   through a cheesecloth veil, through squalls
   of brine and mosquitoes, eyes fixed
as if her looking could keep the poles from falling.

As, as. She cannot push her brush past *as*
   to slip through fissures in the grey masks
   or between the live trees' needles,
'resentful at how tightly they sealed their secrets

from me.' And so she paints this totem as
   a woman grown wooden with grief,
   eyelids drawn down by ropes of tears
gone dry, like limestone wept from a cave's roof,

the ropes pulled taut by teardrop pendulums,
   each with eyelid slits and weakly
   upturned mouth slit: twin parodies
aimed at the one-who-tends-to-smile, *Klee Wyck.*

(Her crest before the long, artless years sank
   landlady into her face: a mask
   'not glad, not sorry, just blank,'
in solid heartwood, live wood's sealed-up corpse.)

* * *

In fact, the totem was no weeping woman.
   It was Sea Chief, whose eyes (not tears)
   climb from their sockets down rope-chains
at night and – perched like buddhas at his feet –

outstare the winking black. Strong lookers, schooled
   to breach a thicker element
   by Frog, whose forelegs hug their sides
while Sea Chief holds the powerful tiller

of his hind legs. Now, Sea Chief's disembodied
   gaze breaks into Emily's eyes
   and seizes the abandoned totem
of her dead self to house her wiser one.

                    * * *

Think of it now as the house pole that it is,
   no 'house of all sorts,' but a lodge
   with cedar-lidded lanterns, twin
beacons in midnight's pastures. Foragers

whose dreamlit browsing sees her through the night.
   She grips the brush: her sight lifts past
   its focal point. She navigates
along the edge of nowhere, sweeps her wrist

in swimming strokes: her brush rides through warm blue
   currents the sun fingers in sea
   and sky, towards cold blue ones the moon
glances along the bones of fallen cedars.

Deeper and higher than the sea-mist reaches,
   it rides where salmon leap upstream
   to spawn and die, where raven's breast
stiffens hooding its brood from its last storm.

* * *

She rode the current Sea Chief's eyes see through –
   saltwater source, long as the chain
   of breath. The waters seep into
heartwood through thickest bark, the salt can burn,

for each drop hugs its constant opposite fire
   which seasons where it stings. Knifeblade
   current that splits the shell-strewn shore
to bury itself in the sea's unfolding life.

Goodly Cedar

It shall bring forth boughs ... and be a goodly cedar: and under it shall dwell all fowl of every wing; in the shadow of the branches thereof shall they dwell. (Ezekiel 17:23)

1. As in my first treehouse, in primeval
   East Brooklyn – my father's cedar
wardrobe. I reach up, swing its double doors,
   and tarzan over the panel

   into a fragrant gloom, landing softly
   on my nest of rumpled flannel
beneath the arching, hollow limbs of wool
   and cotton. Then I coax the stiff

   plank gates inwards and hunker down, squatter
   in paradise. Ruby-throated
light breaks, treetop-distant, through two keyholes.
   Wings of water-dazzle flutter

   downwards: half bird, I paddle their slipstreams;
   half fish, I breathe them in. Later,
hauled up at bedtime from the fenced concrete
   beneath my window, I embrace

   the blanket, nuzzle in its cedar smell,
   and fall asleep dreaming myself
higher than treetops, spreading wings, flying
   over a city growing small.

2. Oh, how we work to do what comes to them
   at the flick of an instinct: flight,
to us so much premeditated metal,
   is the light water where they swim

   with all their feathers on; song rises through
   their throats as easily as air
bubbles up from under water; colour
   springs from dark shells of insects who

vanish inside them. Envious, we paint
   them with our words, coating the dove
in mourning, dribbling red sealant over
   the waxwing's wingtips, laying slate

on the small junco. Escaping our shades,
   they withdraw into airy lives
splashed with light, absorbed and unreflective,
   too dawn-drenched to dream of Eden.

3. Grey in my hair matches the slate of split
   cedar rails in the overgrown
orchard. Every summer, we've hauled them down,
   trudging like horses between shafts,

two under each arm, to transplant the fence
   (itself fenced now in forests of
apple, maple, and ash) along the curved
   slope that will mark where wilderness

leaves off, and beds and lawns begin: a rough
   circle embracing house, garden,
the pond's smooth inlaid blue. Now, after ten
   years watching weeds and mortgages

rise every spring to flood out of control,
   we've sold, and yet we still work madly
to salvage the last ten or twelve panels
   of fence. A stubborn gravity

keeps them unraised, like the missing strokes
   an artist needs to lift white paint
into clouds, or notes a songwriter
   searches for, to raise the music

he feels along the soundboard of his heart.
Late August lowers our pond's clouds
and drains light from our evenings: now we pound
spikes by flashlight, need to spread tarps

to blanket saws and spades from heavy dew.
When I cut wedges from spoiled rails
to chink the panels straight, and my sawblade
bites into the grizzled cedar,

sweet fumes from childhood rise up from the cuts,
hover on the damp air, and make
a fragrant haven in the growing dark.
Which, with days of rain, defeats us.

4. On our last afternoon, cedar perfume
fills the rain-drenched house. I carry
the birdhouse my son's indoor carpentry
has coaxed from scraps of fresh lumber

and mount it on our last, untrimmed fence post –
sentinel over no man's land.
I haven't gone to see it since. I find
my thoughts stray to its visitors,

finches or warblers who will huddle down,
as rain drenches their light-winged roof,
and breathe (not knowing that they breathe) perfume,
and perch along the fence staves (notes

in music they can't read) and never see
the cedar dried and grey; yet in
their short flights make complete circles a man
should know better than to envy.

Throat Singers

Silas Kayakjuak begins with stone –
two lead-solid loaves, doorstop-sized –
because he wants to anchor this moment,
to keep the wind from blowing it out to sea.

Green stone. Not jade's Arctic-water pallor
or the icy aurora of emerald: a yellower green
mottled with sunlight. Skin of a basking frog,
ochre carpet of pondweed he floats on.

So, Silas has already compromised,
straying from the northern scene. His green
softens, to pastel positive, the shore
where two Inuit women face the dead black

of an Arctic winter. The lumpish stone, however,
embodies the way their parkas' avalanche buries
any hint of chiseled southern sleekness:
they stand more like a pair of carved muskoxen.

He's caught their closeness too, as if hinged
along one side and folded nearly flat,
singing into each other's mouths, each needing
to feel the other's rhythm and breath-warmth

to free her own voice. He can never hope
to catch their song: waves of sound, all vowel,
freed from the icy stops of consonants,
far too quick for stone, flow into the wind.

Yet, Silas knows stone can never sing,
just as he knows the greenest stone won't flower.
He knows the way to anchor this moment
is not to pin it down, but to call it up

by mooring it in the dark inside the green stone.
  Deeper than night's dark, sister to that dark
inside ourselves crying out for the light
  of song – the dark these sisters stare into

down each other's throats: dark of the soul's
  caverns, source of the fragile art (so sleek
the eye can't make it out, the ear almost
  at once loses it) that flies from their lips.

He drills two throat-holes deep into the stone
  to carve an absence that recalls the most
sublime presence – not song, not greenery:
  warm breath's white flowers floating in the air.

A Canoe for Tim

When you walk this earth you must walk carefully:
underneath your feet is the knife's edge, and you
could fall off this world. (Haida proverb)

1. Or be cut to pieces by the blade, the way
   our rented canoe, beached safely (so we thought)
   fell under rather than off the stormwaves' axe.

   We couldn't believe how little the bits were –
   sticks whittled from thick wood of thwart and gunnel,
   and the hull's light sounding board chopped fine as rice.

   That summer, you both learned to paddle: artful
   dipping by eight-year-old girl, in time with flat-
   bladed splashes from four-year-old brother, both

   enthralled by the glide of wood over water
   in whispered quickness less like other human
   boating than like the fogs lifting around us.

   Gone with them, as thoroughly as the canoe's
   knifeblade wake dissolved behind us, the children
   you were then – only two shadows surviving

   in a veneer thinner than paper to haunt
   this photograph: Short Man beside Giant Wife.
   They stand arm in arm, both dwarfed (and overcome

   with giggles) inside their joke, their parents' clothes,
   put on to show who's boss, floppy sweatshirts – hers
   a knee-length dress, his a gown – with running shoes

   so oversized the thin legs lodge like paddles
   upright in canvas canoes. The camera
   moors them forever at mid-stream on the deck's

flow of cedar planks and the knife-edged currents
  of blackness running between them. Who's boss now?
    Not the camera, which has let the real flow

escape, the slipping into and out of clothes
  and figures, fits of giggles and selves, its lens
    focused on trappings, ghosts of the aperture.

As if you could save sunlight in a black box,
  or wield a paddle anchored in an oarlock,
    or carve history into water's marble.

2. In the early thirties, as Europe's butchers
    sharpened their knives for slaughter, the OED
      first published the definition of 'canoe'

  that stood for nearly sixty years while cities
    fell and buried children: 'any rude craft in
      which uncivilized people go upon the

  water; most savages use paddles instead
    of oars.' In those same years before the man-made
      storm and mushroom cloud, the Salvation Army

  raised an old totem pole at a children's camp
    in Illinois: museum surplus, the pole
      (let it stand here for everything uprooted

  by the savagery of lettered ignorance)
    once stood before the coastal village portal
      of the Haida craftsmen whose hands worked it from

  fragrant, straight-grained cedar with the same curved knives
    they used to carve their cedar houses, cradles,
      canoes, and paddles. Artful with wood, artful

on water, 'the good people' nearly fell off
this world, driven to the edge by Europe's push,
suspended in *yahgu nass* – the middle house –

until pulled back by hands cutting old designs
in fresh wood, carvers raising new coastal stands
of totems for the portals of Haida Gwaii.

3. All of them flow, rivers of figures braiding,
mingling or overlapping, gliding in and
out of each other's runnels, metamorphic

and fleet as northern lights or as two small frogs
that leap, near the base of one pole, from the ears
of Sea Bear. He yawns and swallows a dogfish

head first (tail flukes protruding), and his thick brows
fuse with the downward head of Killer Whale, whose
dorsal fin sits between the knees of a man

shown upside-down, riding on Killer Whale's back
beneath a tall woman grasping Eagle's curled
talons (a hair seal peeking from between them).

From above Eagle's wings the pectoral fins
of another whale (whose folded-up hind end
provides the hair seal with a floppy bonnet)

point upwards towards the summit: Raven's head, crowned
with three ring-hatted watchmen, their feet one with
his human ears, their eyes taking in the sea.

Stand underneath and look up: the edging blue
dissolves in shimmers as, upright, a canoe
heads for the islanded waters of the sky.

FOUR

Insides/Outsides: Five Haiku

Creation

Beneath their duvet
(one side blue, the other black)
bright-eyed stars dream on.

Tomatoes on the Table

At six, between the
sheets' white silence and the streets',
red bells wake my eyes.

Near a Subway Station

One shoe in the street
and breath over the grating
calling Orpheus.

Gerald Trimming Hawthorn

Flint-barked barbed hedger,
your brief white word-blossoms yield
small red stone-filled fruits.

The Inside Rail of the Indoor Track

knows nothing of in-
wardness compared to that ship
whose deck it surrounds.

Chink

The sun raises a ruckus on Yonge Street:
a waterfall of bits of glass fractures
infinitely faster than you can say its sound
chink-chink-chink-chink-chink-chink-chink-chink-chink-chink
a well of chirping spurts from the black rift
between the brick facades of two storefronts
as the first shaft of light this cold spring morning
shivers tiny diamonds in the bricks,
the wall a blinding live minefield of glitter.

Come back an hour later, light's rolling boil
dims to a simmer, you can stand to look
into the source of the ruckus: three-finger-wide
black chink running from sidewalk to roofline.
At random all along it, woolly muddles
of string, hair, leaf-stems, dried grass, dingy feathers
bundled wherever mortar between bricks
oozed out and froze into enough grey ledge
to cantilever nests across the gap.

This rubble-strewn, ramshackle tenement,
teetering in an upturned canyon's blackness,
houses the impoverished choristers
of morning. In chatters still, they flicker from
the narrow chink as inexhaustibly
as silk scarves out of a magician's fist.
How do they live? What hard grain do they peck
from concrete? Do the leafless hydro-pole
branches they fill bear unimagined fruit?

Back in the chink, beyond the scope of eyes
or ears because so deeply woven with
its nothingness, other sparrows must wait,
warming the small eggs. To believe their few
teaspoons of heat will yield enough fire
to crack those pebbles into song and flight
is no more difficult than to believe
the sparrows' chink-chink breaks open the night,
their ruckus raises the sun on Yonge Street.

Winter Fruit

Look at them, filling every vacant blue niche
    with ripe clusters of pure transparency,
abundance such that not one more fruit would fit
    among the leafless branches, yet each group
has room to grow and never bruise its neighbour.
    I looked through them for years, thinking winter
a fruitless white waste, until water trained me
    in their subtle habits.
                            The more you knew
of earth, the more unlikely such emergence:
    under the dark loam that softened in spring
to let the plough comb through, under the packed clay
    that locked something of summer warmth in its
brick-solid oven, so like stone it could snap
    a probing spade, drier to sight than stone
because it lacked the river-shimmer of quartz,
    unearthly coolness flowed.
                            It bubbled up
between two overlapping tables of shale
    that, slanted at a low embankment, made
a partly opened doorway for the water
    to slip through, nearly perfectly disguised
as nothing, at a distance invisible
    but for the darkening where its shadow seeped
into the stone – and settled.
                            Freed, the water
    itself flowed shadowless as globed crystal
spilling from snow-brimmed caves when the winter sun
    distills white's brilliant essence. Pure outpour
undimmed by even a vapoured density,
    it was the clear soul of the close-knit earth
that filtered it, a fulfillment of the light
    rising from knotted substance the way stars
breed from the blackest night.

                    Or as winter fruit
     concentrates ripened silence in blue space
between branches. You can't mistake the clearness
     for death or dearth: this fruit harbours the seeds
of flowering speech. You reach out with your voice,
     put your mouth around it and bite into
the yielding stillness at sound's core. You tap
     a river cooler than spring water, more
remote, feel the north star roll
                         along your tongue.

Mining for Sun

At this remove from the yellow flower
that blooms along the sky's coast every day,
it takes some doing to extract the light.

Begin, as you stand in the unyielding
shade of a highrise's northern rockface,
by planting an explosive charge under

your assumptions: nobody will see you,
and the resulting blast will not disturb
one grain of the soot that has come to rest

on the stone window ledge above your head,
yet it will sink shafts through what seems concrete
in walls and sidewalks, amazing them with new

slants on a bright idea as old as time.
This tunnelling goes deeper than the site's
present foundation, leading back beyond

the glint of morning on the mansard roof
of a brick dry-goods shop, beyond gaslight
threading a frame hotel's iron railings.

Yet, without moving one step out of now,
you can fathom the depth of every shaft.
Touch the wall's sandstone facing, and your hand

fingers the same slow pulse that beat among
its molecules before the glacial lake
pressed them from crystal grains of mountains – once

all incandescent liquid like the dawn.
Deep in the steel beam of the new cliffside
rising across the street, atoms circle

to the same firedance that coaxed their gleam
out of the rock when they were reimmersed,
by a blast furnace, in the melting air

that played over the earth when the whole world
was a red ocean, rippling with first light.
The blacktopped roadbed also raises waves

of shimmer, in an inexhaustible
winging-back-up of light that sleeps within
earth's spinning chrysalis: look you wake it.

If you still need a hand, the street signal
flashes high five to guide you, as the small
beacons of tail lights aim to fire you up;

the locust tree, its claim pitched in a square
of shade dark as the soil around its roots,
quarries light from the air, urging you on

with bursts of green applause from its grey bark,
while, at the curb, the fire hydrant waits
for you to see it as a capped fountain,

all latent gleam and billow. Dive into
its rainbow. Mine a new world that's always
been waiting for your sun to rise from it.

The White Horse

1. This horse, not only tamed but humbled, rests
on a desk-pad under clear
plastic, part of a scene that dominates
the hall that stables the original oil.

Reproduced, belittled, Constable's stream
is housebroken, its stretch of willow knit
into a parsley sprig. My thumb
eclipses the thatched roof's tarnished sun;

a plump bee could obliterate the horse.
Yet, doing so, it would draw down
chaos on the whole miniature world,
since – even on a basement desk remote

from Constable's sky-rearing herds of clouds –
only the white horse has the power to keep
tiny blackbirds aloft, and boughs
lifting blurred trunks (about to melt and slip

into deeps that already possess their shadows,
the inexorable slow pull
of lodestone earth drowning the water weeds
and powdering the marl on the tow-path).

What gives the horse such power? His legs, unlike
the pillared muscles of a real workhorse,
are artful supposition, blocked
by the prow of the barge that ferries him, his eyes

blinkered and turned away from us. It is
the radiance of his hide, whiteness
so strong it makes the painting's other whites
pale in comparison. It focuses

the lustre of the prow's bleached wood, the sheen
of stucco on the house facade, the pearls
that bubble where the stream resists
the barge's push: the way an arrowhead

targets a feathered shaft's lift, giving it
an edge to take on gravity.
The black straps of his harness concentrate –
by underlining how it cannot be

reined in – the white hide's fury, an unearthly
outburst of sunlit snow against a landscape
steeped in July haze. It is he,
and not the bargeman with his pin-sized pole,

who drives the sluggish lighter through the dark,
syrupy water: dynamo and source
that won't run down or dry, art's work
(unnatural and necessary) horse.

2. Sometimes nature can come so close, it breathes
down the white horse's neck. When snow
sets up a canvas in thin air up north
and pelts it all night with white tracer arrows,

sunrise unveils a landscape suddenly
focused on one design. Snow's work resists
the magnetism of decay
which cracked browned earth, drew it into fissures

and burdened water, deepening hillside flumes.
Snow buttresses the wood's pillars,
shores up eroded banks, plugs rifts, transforms
a path's raked timber planking to the sheer

unbroken white ascent of feathered flights.
Enameller of baskets (run-down since
the last harvest), freelance painter,
no job too small, even the seams between bricks.

Snow's coat won't take after the first spring thaws
dilute it; yet, until then, if
snow's untamed white horse leaps onto your house,
his icicle-fringed mane will raise the roof.

3. That white horse can't survive an hour on King Street,
   dismembered like a cast-off costume horse –
   front, back, each with its own dark fate.
   Salt bites into the galloping forelegs

   that light on asphalt, chews them to brown mash,
   then spits out morsels for the cars
   to forage on, weeping messes that splash
   wheelrims and congeal there layer by layer

   until their own weight breaks them loose in chunks
   of iron-grey meteorite. The splayed
   hindquarters and the steaming flanks
   that hover over sidewalks, neon-dyed

   in the electric glare, come shivering
   down to hit the wet pavement,
   a million tiny arrow-sparks bound where
   nothing will ever light them up again.

4. Deep in unnatural afternoon shadow
   thrown by King Street's leafless, banked ravine,
   I walked its dried-up riverbed
   out of touch with the sky, and found a sign:

nothing come from above, like snow – no steed
white-winged and apocalyptic –
no icon with his right hand pointed upward
like someone hailing a celestial taxi.

It was a simple, horizontal sign,
an arrow pointing at a one-way street –
anonymous and unrefined
as horses painted on the endless night

of prehistoric cave walls; yet it called
beyond the limits of its fixed
pursuit. It voiced pure whiteness through the shade,
clear passage through solidities, upsurge

accelerated by the black-veiled rim
the white arrow split in its even flight.
I felt it drive me on, image
of something deep inside: the same white heat

that fired the first artists when they gave
new warmth to charcoal, grinding it
with their own teeth, mixing it with saliva
to form the pigment that would animate

the senseless walls, raised to life by black horses.
Their shapes – like photographic negatives –
reduce, reverse, but still express
the potency of the white horse alive

inside them. That white horse carries us through
the dark, urging a route one-way,
earthbound, yet aimed beyond nature's view.
Unique and common, never-landing arrow.

Bakery Specials

The window displays two kinds of special.

The still variety, arrayed on three
receding, step-like shelves covered with green
construction paper and a carpeting
of paper lace, offers the more opaque
delight, an edible architecture
of marble slabs, white-stuccoed gingerbread,
glazed pastry shells ranged behind chocolate squares,
and, cantilevered over wicker vaults,
buttressed pavilions of thin-walled baguette.

The other kind of special lets light through
and can't be bought or eaten, ghostly treats
that move, as if translucency freed them
from stony sleep: beside the tray of brownies,
a traffic light blinks green; nodding buses
and cars waken and roll across the ledge
of the first step, while underneath this road –
a highway that the window elevates
without visible pillars – little people
pass by; one of them, swerving, slides open
a loaf-high telephone booth's rippling fold,
pauses, then aims a microscopic coin.

This captive, miniature city signs
its own exotic languages – YAWA WOT
beckons from thin posts, and a square of red
pinpoints flashes TIAW at the corner –
and holds to its own geometric rules:
a highrise climbs from the top shelf on stilts
of rigid, vertical aluminum
panels that go soft when they reach the heights
contained within the bakery's transom,
wavering, billowing out as if glimpsed
behind an oven's rising scrim of heat.

No matter where you look, there's such abundance
the hungry eye can't choose between the two
varieties, but the window never
demands we choose: it folds today's specials
into each other, as the baker folds
airy meringue into a thicker batter.
Two men walk lightly over a fruit flan
while, near them, a bright orange moving van
snuggles beside a plate of raised donuts;
a streetlamp rises like some climber's flag
from an iced cupcake's maraschino peak;
over them all, in the sky's polished glow,
the vapour trails of four flourescent tubes
flying in close formation streak into
the infinite opaques of the bakeshop.

Daily Bread

We have cried often when we have given them the little victualling we
had to give them; we had to shake them, and they have fallen to sleep
with the victuals in their mouths many a time.

> (parent of children working at a textile mill, to an
> 1832 Parliamentary inquiry into child employment)

1. They cry for children too tired to cry for themselves,
   daughters twelve, eleven, eight – eyes
   shutting down as a grate's banked coals shut down
   at midnight, in the rising damp called 'home.'
   Too tired to eat after eighteen hours feeding
   looms whose steel teeth grind insatiably,
   the girls will be offered up again at dawn.

   Yet they are the lucky ones, to work where skylights
   hold swatches of the unaffordable blue.
   Imagine these girls' mine-trapped cousins, hauling
   black rocks on sledges up tunnels of black air:
   half-undressed, belted, harnessed, saturated
   with the oil-blackened water they crawl through
   pumping 'the lifeblood of British industry.'

   Flogged for talking, Margaret Comeley, aged
   nine, can sometimes close her mouth around
   a piece of muffin – if she manages
   to keep it from the rats, 'so ravenous
   they eat the corks out of our oil-flasks.'
   Sarah Gooder fills her mouth with song
   'when I've light, but not in the dark; I dare not then.'

2. Here is a working girl so filled with light
   she is pure song: her sun-bright bodice shines
   in counterpoint with her blue overskirt,
   and, from her forehead's crescent of white linen,
   tapering light blazes a white path
   down arms and wrists to folds of spread blue cloth,
   like moonlight piloting the tide's refrains.

   A Dutch milkmaid, Tanneke Everpoel,
   lucky enough to live in the Delft house
   where Vermeer's eye and brush could catch the spill
   of morning light as her brief peacefulness
   brimmed over, serves here as a celebrant –
   bread heaped up on the altar-like table,
   wine transubstantiated into milk

   whose brilliance seems the source of the room's light
   she pours forever from the earthenware's
   black core. His pose; yet – all hers – underneath it
   (and signalled in her fixed eyes' unconcern
   for the beholder) such complete immersion
   in what she does, that she *is* all she does
   and it is she, this offering-up of day.

   And he? When he was forty, the Sun King
   invaded Holland. No one wanted art.
   In debt to his baker for three years' worth of bread,
   Vermeer, according to his widow, falling
   'into a frenzy,' passed 'from being healthy'
   in 'a day or a day and a half ... to being dead,'
   'the very great burden of his children ... so taken to heart.'

3. Knowing the earth is closer to the sun
   in winter won't revive the street person
   sleeping towards cold death in a bus shelter.
   Bread in a painting won't cure stomach ache.
   So Margaret dragged her great burden of coal
   while Sarah sat terrified in the dark,
   and neither knew Vermeer's poised working girl,

   broke bread with her, shared her breaking light.
   The painting stood by, helpless to save them
   or him, and looking at it now cannot
   help anyone. Yet, it can cry for them,
   as parents take their children's grief to heart:
   the beads of salt, shimmering on the bread
   like diamonds, can be tears the two girls shed

   down where no light sang their preciousness.
   The cradled pitcher's brim can be their hearth,
   since it (and not the sky's cold mine of stars)
   pours out what cannot shelter us, but feeds
   a hunger no daily bread can fill: for light –
   light that, like coal, comes from our earth; hunger
   that, unlike grief, is inexhaustible.

Acknowledgements

Some of these poems (sometimes in earlier versions) appeared originally in *The Antigonish Review, Arc, Canadian Literature, The Fiddlehead, The Malahat Review, The New Quarterly*, the *Newsletter* of the Elizabeth Bishop Society of Nova Scotia, *The Paris Review, Quarry, The Southern Review, Southwest Review, Western Humanities Review, Windsor Review*, and in *Near Finisterre* (Toronto, St. Thomas Poetry Series, 1996) and *Vintage 95* (ed. Linda Rogers, Quarry Press, 1996).

The author is grateful to the editors of the above publications, and to John Donlan for the wonderfully keen eye, ear, and conscience he has brought to the editing of this collection. These poems have also benefited from the kind scrutiny of fellow writers in the Vic group, particularly from suggestions made by Jeffery Donaldson, A.F. Moritz, and Sheldon Zitner.

The Raven epigraph is taken from Peter Goodchild's collection of *Raven Tales* (Chicago Review Press), the Barfield epigraph from *History, Guilt, and Habit* (Wesleyan University Press), and the Bonnefoy epigraph from *The Act and the Place of Poetry* (University of Chicago Press).

Warm and grateful acknowledgement is made to Barbara Kemp for permission to use Robert Kemp's 'Friday Night' on the cover, and to Timothy Reibetanz for the author photo.

Biographical Note

John Reibetanz was born in New York City, and grew up in the eastern United States and Canada. He studied at the City University of New York and Princeton University, and has written essays on Elizabethan drama and on modern and contemporary poetry, as well as a book on *King Lear* and translations of modern German poetry.

His poems have appeared in such magazines as *Poetry* (Chicago), *The Paris Review, Canadian Literature, The Malahat Review*, and *The Fiddlehead*, and twice in the anthology of winning entries to the National Poetry Competition. His earlier collections, *Ashbourn* and *Morning Watch*, were published in the Signal Editions series of Véhicule Press; in 1996, *Midland Swimmer* was published by Brick Books and *Near Finisterre* appeared in the St. Thomas Poetry Series. He is a member of the League of Canadian Poets, and was a finalist for the 1995 National Magazine Awards.

He lives in Toronto and teaches at Victoria College, where in 1989 he received the first Victoria University Teaching Award. His favourite non-literary pursuits are local history, contemporary art, and 1930s jazz.